D1089002

JR. GRAPHIC AMERICAN INVENTORS

GEORGE WASHINGTON CARVER

Jane Gould

PowerKiDS
press

New York

Published in 2013 by The Rosen Publishing Group, Inc.
29 East 21st Street, New York, NY 10010

First Edition

Editor: Joanne Randolph

Book Design: Planman Technologies

Illustrations: Planman Technologies

Library of Congress Cataloging-in-Publication Data

Gould, Jane.

George Washington Carver / by Jane Gould. — 1st ed.

    p. cm. — (Jr. graphic American inventors)

Includes index.

ISBN 978-1-4777-0078-5 (library binding) — ISBN 978-1-4777-0141-6 (pbk.) — ISBN 978-1-4777-0142-3 (6-pack)

1. Carver, George Washington, 1864?-1943—Comic books, strips, etc.—Juvenile literature. 2. African American agriculturists—Biography—Comic books, strips, etc.—Juvenile literature. 3. Agriculturists—United States—Biography—Comic books, strips, etc.—Juvenile literature. 4. African American scientists—Biography—Comic books, strips, etc.—Juvenile literature. 5. African American educators—Biography—Comic books, strips, etc.—Juvenile literature. 6. Peanuts—United States—History—Comic books, strips, etc.—Juvenile literature. 7. Graphic novels. I. Title.

S417.C3G68 2013

630.92—dc23

[B]

2012018689

Manufactured in the United States of America

CPSIA Compliance Information: Batch # W13PK1: For Further Information contact Rosen Publishing, New York, New York at 1-800-237-9932

Contents

Introduction

George Washington Carver was an African American born into slavery during the **Civil War**. Life was hard for all African Americans living at that time, but Carver rose to become one of the most famous scientists in the United States. His work in **agriculture** helped many poor farmers in the South. He is best known for making peanuts a popular food. He also proved that plants could be used to create many **products** that would give people better lives.

Main Characters

 George Washington Carver (1864?–1943) An African American scientist and teacher at Tuskegee Institute, in Tuskegee, Alabama. Carver helped change agriculture in the American South and was known for his work with the peanut.

 Susan and Moses Carver (1812–1910) The white couple who once owned George Washington Carver's mother and who raised him and his brother Jim after the Civil War.

 Henry Ford (1863–1947) The American businessman who created the Ford automobile company.

 Helen and John Milholland (1880s) White friends of Carver's in Iowa who convinced him to go to college.

 Booker T. Washington (1856–1915) The African American president of Tuskegee Institute who invited Carver to start an agriculture program at the school.

 Mariah and Andrew Watkins (1870s) An African American couple who took care of Carver when he first went to school in Neosho, Missouri.

GEORGE WASHINGTON CARVER

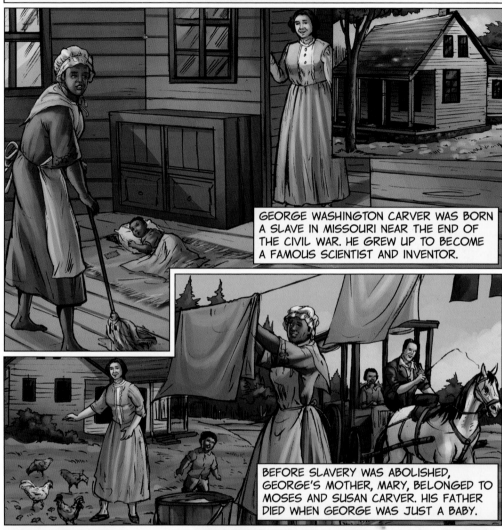

GEORGE WASHINGTON CARVER WAS BORN A SLAVE IN MISSOURI NEAR THE END OF THE CIVIL WAR. HE GREW UP TO BECOME A FAMOUS SCIENTIST AND INVENTOR.

BEFORE SLAVERY WAS ABOLISHED, GEORGE'S MOTHER, MARY, BELONGED TO MOSES AND SUSAN CARVER. HIS FATHER DIED WHEN GEORGE WAS JUST A BABY.

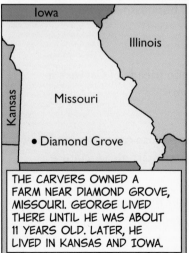

THE CARVERS OWNED A FARM NEAR DIAMOND GROVE, MISSOURI. GEORGE LIVED THERE UNTIL HE WAS ABOUT 11 YEARS OLD. LATER, HE LIVED IN KANSAS AND IOWA.

HERE IS MY BEST HORSE AS A REWARD FOR FINDING GEORGE.

THE CIVIL WAR WAS A DANGEROUS TIME IN MISSOURI. GEORGE AND HIS MOTHER, MARY, WERE KIDNAPPED. MOSES SENT A FRIEND TO FIND THEM. HE FOUND ONLY GEORGE.

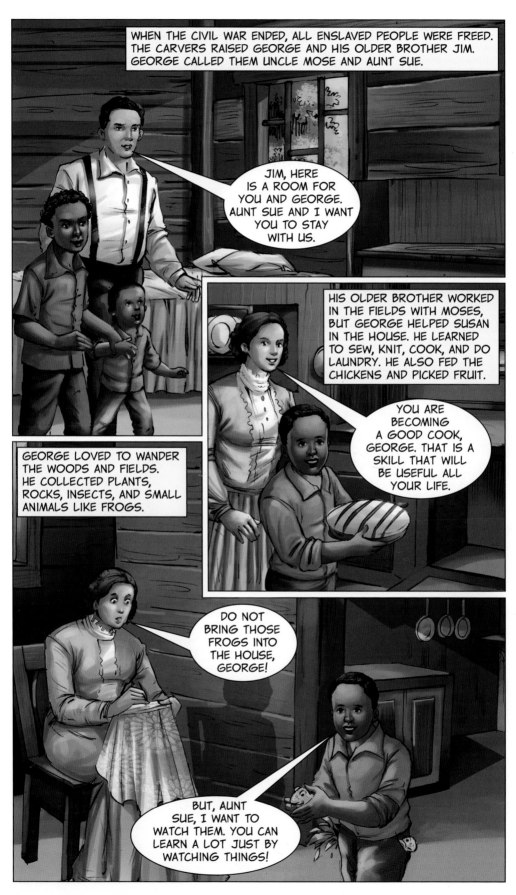

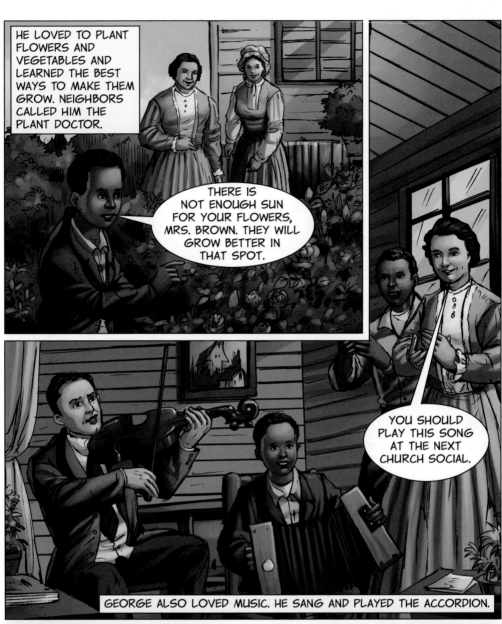

HE LOVED TO PLANT FLOWERS AND VEGETABLES AND LEARNED THE BEST WAYS TO MAKE THEM GROW. NEIGHBORS CALLED HIM THE PLANT DOCTOR.

THERE IS NOT ENOUGH SUN FOR YOUR FLOWERS, MRS. BROWN. THEY WILL GROW BETTER IN THAT SPOT.

YOU SHOULD PLAY THIS SONG AT THE NEXT CHURCH SOCIAL.

GEORGE ALSO LOVED MUSIC. HE SANG AND PLAYED THE ACCORDION.

DO YOU THINK IT LOOKS LIKE THE SUNSET, JIM?

IT LOOKS REAL. I CAN ALMOST HEAR THE CRICKETS CHIRPING.

MOST OF ALL, GEORGE LOVED TO PAINT. HE MADE PAINTS FROM ROOTS AND BERRIES. HE USED TWIGS FOR BRUSHES AND PAINTED ON BOARDS, ROCKS, AND OLD CANS.

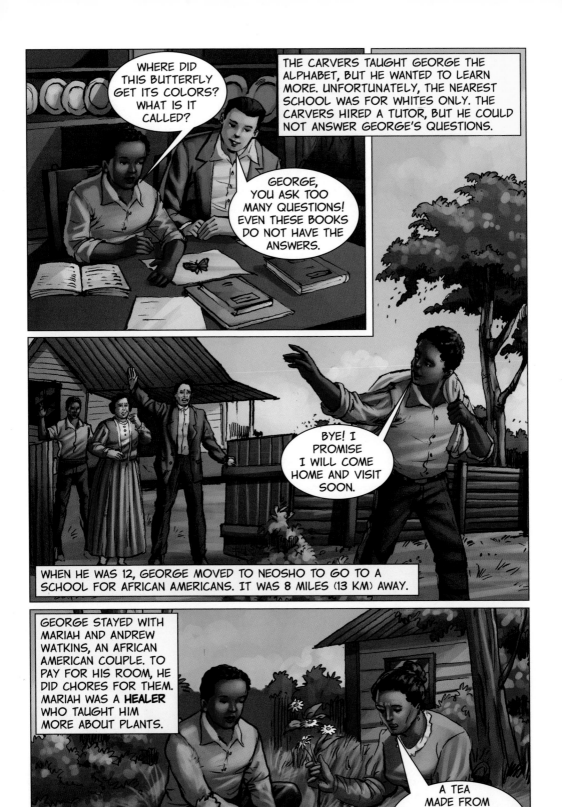

WHERE DID THIS BUTTERFLY GET ITS COLORS? WHAT IS IT CALLED?

THE CARVERS TAUGHT GEORGE THE ALPHABET, BUT HE WANTED TO LEARN MORE. UNFORTUNATELY, THE NEAREST SCHOOL WAS FOR WHITES ONLY. THE CARVERS HIRED A TUTOR, BUT HE COULD NOT ANSWER GEORGE'S QUESTIONS.

GEORGE, YOU ASK TOO MANY QUESTIONS! EVEN THESE BOOKS DO NOT HAVE THE ANSWERS.

BYE! I PROMISE I WILL COME HOME AND VISIT SOON.

WHEN HE WAS 12, GEORGE MOVED TO NEOSHO TO GO TO A SCHOOL FOR AFRICAN AMERICANS. IT WAS 8 MILES (13 KM) AWAY.

GEORGE STAYED WITH MARIAH AND ANDREW WATKINS, AN AFRICAN AMERICAN COUPLE. TO PAY FOR HIS ROOM, HE DID CHORES FOR THEM. MARIAH WAS A **HEALER** WHO TAUGHT HIM MORE ABOUT PLANTS.

A TEA MADE FROM **CHAMOMILE** WILL HELP PEOPLE SLEEP. MINT IS GOOD FOR THE STOMACH.

AFTER A YEAR, GEORGE DECIDED THAT HE HAD LEARNED ALL HE COULD IN NEOSHO. HE WENT TO FORT SCOTT, KANSAS. IN 1879, GEORGE SAW A BLACK MAN KILLED BY A MOB OF WHITES. HE QUICKLY MOVED AGAIN.

GEORGE FOUND A SCHOOL IN OLATHE, KANSAS, WHICH BECAME HIS NEW HOME. HE WAS TOO POOR TO GO TO SCHOOL AS OFTEN AS HE WANTED, AND HE HAD TO WORK.

CAN YOU DELIVER THE CLEAN SHEETS BY TOMORROW?

YES, MA'AM. I WILL HAVE THEM FOR YOU IN THE MORNING.

GEORGE MOVED TO MINNEAPOLIS, KANSAS, IN 1880. HE KEPT GOING TO SCHOOL AND AGAIN STARTED UP A LAUNDRY BUSINESS. HE ALSO ADDED HIS MIDDLE NAME, WASHINGTON.

I AM NOT GETTING MY MAIL.

THERE IS ANOTHER GEORGE CARVER IN TOWN. ADD A MIDDLE NAME SO NO ONE GETS CONFUSED.

THE COLLEGE PRESIDENT SAYS WE WILL NEVER ENROLL **NEGROES** AT THIS SCHOOL.

IN 1885, GEORGE WASHINGTON CARVER APPLIED TO A COLLEGE IN KANSAS. HE WAS ACCEPTED, BUT WHEN HE ARRIVED, HE WAS TURNED AWAY. HE NEVER FORGOT THE **REJECTION**.

SOON AFTER THAT INCIDENT, CARVER BECAME A **HOMESTEADER** IN WESTERN KANSAS. HE LIKED LIVING ON THE PLAINS, BUT IT WAS A HARD LIFE. AFTER A TERRIBLE BLIZZARD IN 1888, HE MOVED TO IOWA.

HOWDY, GEORGE. COULD YOU COME BY TO LOOK AT MY CORN? I NEED YOUR ADVICE.

I WILL COME BY SOON. I JUST WANT TO DRAW THESE PLANTS WHILE THE LIGHT IS BRIGHT.

CARVER WORKED AS A COOK IN WINTERSET, IOWA. HE BECAME FRIENDS WITH HELEN AND JOHN MILHOLLAND. THEY CONVINCED HIM TO APPLY TO SIMPSON COLLEGE.

I AM WORRIED THAT I WILL GO TO THE COLLEGE, AND THEY WILL TURN ME AWAY.

I KNOW THAT THIS SCHOOL WILL NOT CARE ABOUT THE COLOR OF YOUR SKIN.

CARVER WAS THE SECOND AFRICAN AMERICAN TO GO TO SIMPSON. TO EARN MONEY, HE TOOK IN LAUNDRY. PEOPLE AT THE SCHOOL LIKED HIM AND HELPED HIM WHEN THEY COULD.

GEORGE, I GOT A NEW CHAIR. I THOUGHT YOU MIGHT LIKE MY OLD ONE.

GEORGE, YOU LOVE NATURE AND PAINT IT BEAUTIFULLY. I THINK, THOUGH, THAT YOU CAN USE YOUR TALENTS FOR GREATER THINGS.

AT SIMPSON, CARVER STUDIED ART. HIS ART TEACHER KNEW THAT HE LOVED PLANTS. SHE SUGGESTED THAT HE STUDY AGRICULTURE, WHICH COULD LEAD TO A USEFUL CAREER.

I HAVE MET SO MANY POOR FARMERS WHO NEED HELP. MAYBE AGRICULTURE WOULD BE A BETTER WAY TO USE MY EDUCATION.

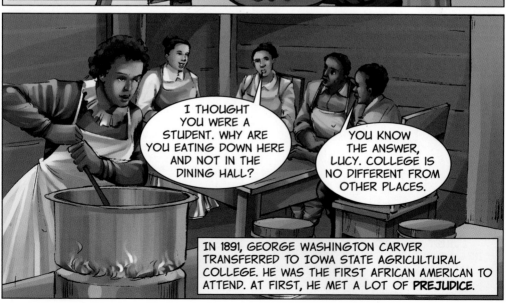

I THOUGHT YOU WERE A STUDENT. WHY ARE YOU EATING DOWN HERE AND NOT IN THE DINING HALL?

YOU KNOW THE ANSWER, LUCY. COLLEGE IS NO DIFFERENT FROM OTHER PLACES.

IN 1891, GEORGE WASHINGTON CARVER TRANSFERRED TO IOWA STATE AGRICULTURAL COLLEGE. HE WAS THE FIRST AFRICAN AMERICAN TO ATTEND. AT FIRST, HE MET A LOT OF **PREJUDICE**.

WASHINGTON BECAME A TEACHER AND LATER SERVED AS THE PRESIDENT OF TUSKEGEE. HE THOUGHT AFRICAN AMERICANS NEEDED TO LEARN SKILLS SUCH AS SEWING AND CONSTRUCTION WORK.

THE SCHOOL OPENED WITH 30 STUDENTS IN 1881. THERE WERE FEW BUILDINGS, AND SOME WERE ONLY SHACKS.

IF YOU LEARN A USEFUL TRADE AND WORK HARD, YOU CAN HAVE A GOOD LIFE.

WASHINGTON WANTED TO OFFER AGRICULTURE CLASSES. CARVER AGREED TO DIRECT THE PROGRAM.

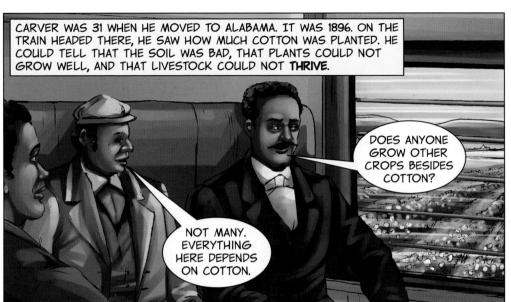

CARVER WAS 31 WHEN HE MOVED TO ALABAMA. IT WAS 1896. ON THE TRAIN HEADED THERE, HE SAW HOW MUCH COTTON WAS PLANTED. HE COULD TELL THAT THE SOIL WAS BAD, THAT PLANTS COULD NOT GROW WELL, AND THAT LIVESTOCK COULD NOT **THRIVE**.

DOES ANYONE GROW OTHER CROPS BESIDES COTTON?

NOT MANY. EVERYTHING HERE DEPENDS ON COTTON.

TUSKEGEE'S STUDENTS DID NOT WANT TO BE FARMERS, LIKE THEIR PARENTS. FARMING WAS HARD WORK, LINKED WITH SLAVERY, AND IT PAID LITTLE. SOON, THOUGH, CARVER STARTED GETTING MORE STUDENTS.

MY FAMILY FARMED WHEN THEY WERE ENSLAVED. I WANT A BETTER LIFE.

THAT'S TRUE, BUT I HEAR DR. CARVER IS A GOOD TEACHER.

I WONDER IF WE REALLY CAN CHANGE THINGS.

HERE IS SOME RUBBER TUBING AND A GRATER!

I FOUND SOME BOTTLES AND CUPS, SIR.

THAT SHOULD HELP. I AM GLAD I BROUGHT MY MICROSCOPE.

TUSKEGEE HAD NO MONEY FOR NEW BUILDINGS, AND THE OLD SHACKS LEAKED. AT FIRST, CARVER DID NOT EVEN HAVE REAL SCIENTIFIC EQUIPMENT FOR HIS LAB.

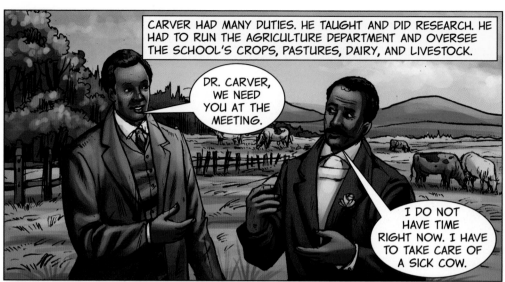

CARVER HAD MANY DUTIES. HE TAUGHT AND DID RESEARCH. HE HAD TO RUN THE AGRICULTURE DEPARTMENT AND OVERSEE THE SCHOOL'S CROPS, PASTURES, DAIRY, AND LIVESTOCK.

DR. CARVER, WE NEED YOU AT THE MEETING.

I DO NOT HAVE TIME RIGHT NOW. I HAVE TO TAKE CARE OF A SICK COW.

YOU ARE ASKING TOO MUCH!

IT'S NO MORE THAN I ASK OF MYSELF.

CARVER AND WASHINGTON DID NOT ALWAYS GET ALONG. HOWEVER, THEY HAD GREAT RESPECT FOR EACH OTHER.

CARVER TOOK HIS STUDENTS ON HIKES TO STUDY NATURE. HE ALSO CREATED A GARDEN WHERE HE COULD TEST CROPS.

LOOK ABOUT YOU. TAKE HOLD OF THE THINGS THAT ARE HERE. LET THEM TALK TO YOU. YOU LEARN TO TALK TO THEM.

EVERY MONTH, THE SCHOOL OFFERED A PROGRAM TO TEACH FARMERS HOW TO TAKE CARE OF THE EARTH AND THEIR PLANTS. THE SCHOOL EVEN GAVE COOKING DEMONSTRATIONS AND EXPLAINED HOW TO PLAN MEALS.

CAN YOUR EXTRA TOMATOES. THEN YOU WILL HAVE TOMATOES IN THE WINTER.

MANY POOR FARMERS COULD NOT COME TO TUSKEGEE, SO CARVER DESIGNED A "MOVEABLE SCHOOL." THIS WAS A WAGON THAT CARRIED INFORMATION, SEEDS, PLANTS, AND EQUIPMENT TO FARMERS AROUND THE STATE.

LET ME SHOW YOU SOME OF THE PLANTS WE GREW IN TUSKEGEE. YOU CAN GROW THEM HERE, TOO.

CARVER KNEW THAT THE SOIL IN THE SOUTH WAS BAD BECAUSE FARMERS PLANTED ONLY ONE CROP, COTTON. COTTON TOOK ALL THE **NUTRIENTS** OUT OF THE SOIL AND MADE IT WORSE EVERY YEAR.

THIS SOIL IS FROM A COTTON FIELD. IT HAS NO NUTRIENTS. NOTHING WILL GROW FROM IT.

HOW CAN THE SOUTH FEED ITS PEOPLE IF ALL IT GROWS IS COTTON?

FEW FOOD CROPS WERE GROWN, AND THERE WAS LITTLE LIVESTOCK. PEOPLE SUFFERED FROM POOR NUTRITION.

THESE PEANUT PLANTS WILL PUT NUTRIENTS BACK INTO THE SOIL. THEY WILL FEED YOUR FAMILY, TOO.

AFTER YOU HARVEST, USE THE LEFTOVER PARTS OF THE PLANTS TO MAKE **COMPOST**.

CARVER SHOWED FARMERS THAT CROP **ROTATION** WOULD HELP THE SOIL. INSTEAD OF GROWING COTTON EVERY YEAR, ONE YEAR, THEY COULD GROW PEANUTS. ANOTHER YEAR, THEY COULD GROW SWEET POTATOES.

THIS WILL SAVE US FROM HAVING TO BUY **FERTILIZER**.

WE HAVE LOTS OF CHICKEN **MANURE** WE CAN ADD, TOO.

TO MAKE THE LAND EVEN MORE **FERTILE**, CARVER USED COMPOST MADE FROM ROTTING PLANTS AND LEAVES. HE ALSO USED ANIMAL MANURE.

LOOK AT THIS COTTON! WITH THE MAGNIFYING GLASS, YOU CAN SEE THE WEEVILS.

THERE ARE NO WEEVILS ON OUR **HYBRID**, DR. CARVER!

CARVER EVEN CREATED A NEW TYPE OF COTTON PLANT, CALLED CARVER'S HYBRID. IT WAS LESS LIKELY TO BE INFECTED BY INSECTS CALLED BOLL WEEVILS, WHICH ATE THE PUFFY COTTON ON THE PLANTS.

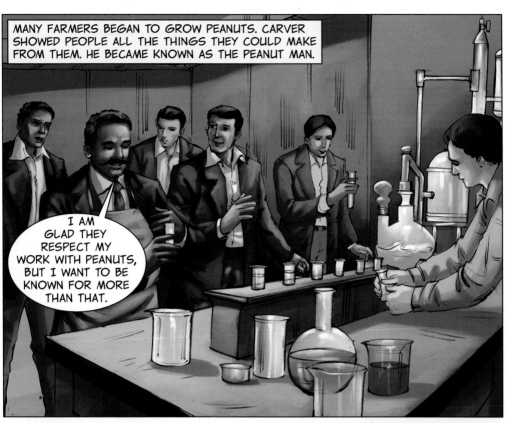

MANY FARMERS BEGAN TO GROW PEANUTS. CARVER SHOWED PEOPLE ALL THE THINGS THEY COULD MAKE FROM THEM. HE BECAME KNOWN AS THE PEANUT MAN.

I AM GLAD THEY RESPECT MY WORK WITH PEANUTS, BUT I WANT TO BE KNOWN FOR MORE THAN THAT.

CARVER MADE MORE THAN 300 DIFFERENT PRODUCTS FROM PEANUTS, INCLUDING OIL, MILK, PAINT, DYES, PAPER, FLOUR, PLASTIC, SOAP, COSMETICS, AND **BIOFUEL**.

LOOK AT ALL THE FOODS I MADE FROM PEANUTS, EVERYTHING FROM SOUP TO DESSERT!

YUM, PEANUT BRITTLE!

BULLETIN NO. 31   JUNE, 1925

HOW TO GROW THE PEANUT

And 105 Ways of Preparing It For Human Consumption
(Fourth Edition)

EXPERIMENT STATION
TUSKEGEE NORMAL and INDUSTRIAL INSTITUTE
TUSKEGEE INSTITUTE, ALABAMA

By
GEO. W. CARVER, M. S. AGR.
Director

HE ALSO CREATED 160 SWEET POTATO PRODUCTS AND MADE PAINT, OIL, CHEESE, FLOUR, COFFEE, AND FUEL, ALL FROM SOYBEANS. HE EVEN PRINTED PAMPHLETS TO EXPLAIN WAYS PEOPLE COULD GROW AND COOK FOOD.

PROFESSOR CARVER, MY COMPANY WANTS TO MAKE AND SELL YOUR PRODUCTS.

I AM NOT A BUSINESSMAN, BUT I WOULD LIKE TO SEE MY WORK BEING PUT TO GOOD USE.

CARVER FOUND **INDUSTRIAL** USES FOR FARM PRODUCTS, AND COMPANIES WANTED TO **MANUFACTURE** HIS FOODS AND COSMETICS. ALTHOUGH CARVER'S WORK MADE HIM FAMOUS, HE NEVER MADE MUCH MONEY FROM IT.

GENTLEMEN, THE FLOUR IN THIS FOOD COMES FROM PEANUTS AND SWEET POTATOES.

MAYBE PEOPLE COULD USE IT INSTEAD OF WHEAT FLOUR.

IN 1918, CARVER WENT TO WASHINGTON, D.C. THE DEPARTMENT OF AGRICULTURE THOUGHT SOME OF HIS FOOD PRODUCTS COULD END FOOD SHORTAGES DURING WORLD WAR I.

BUT THIS MAN IS OUR FEATURED SPEAKER!

SIR, NEGROES ARE NOT ALLOWED ON THIS ELEVATOR. IT IS FOR WHITES ONLY.

DESPITE CARVER'S FAME, HE STILL FACED RACIAL PREJUDICE. IN 1920, HE WAS THE MAIN SPEAKER AT A MEETING FOR THE PEANUT INDUSTRY. HE HAD TO RIDE IN THE BUILDING'S FREIGHT ELEVATOR.

IN 1921, CARVER WAS ASKED TO SPEAK TO THE US HOUSE OF REPRESENTATIVES. THE PEANUT INDUSTRY WANTED CARVER TO EXPLAIN WHY IT WAS IMPORTANT TO GROW PEANUTS IN AMERICA.

PROFESSOR CARVER, YOU HAVE ONLY 10 MINUTES TO SPEAK.

I BROUGHT SOME DELICIOUS FOOD MADE FROM PEANUTS. I AM SORRY YOU CANNOT TASTE IT, BUT I WILL DESCRIBE IT TO YOU.

CARVER SHOWED THE CONGRESSIONAL REPRESENTATIVES THE FOOD, COFFEE, DYES, AND FACE CREAM HE MADE FROM PEANUTS. HE SPOKE FOR ALMOST AN HOUR, AND THE PEANUT INDUSTRY GOT THE SUPPORT IT WANTED.

SCIENCE WILL COME UP WITH EVEN MORE WAYS TO USE THESE PLANTS. ONE DAY, WE MAY NOT NEED TO EAT MEAT OR RUN CARS ON GASOLINE.

I AM PROUD TO RECEIVE THIS HONORARY DOCTOR OF SCIENCE DEGREE FROM MY OLD COLLEGE, ESPECIALLY BECAUSE THE AWARD IS FOR THE WORK I DID WITH FARMERS.

AS CARVER'S FAME GREW, HE RECEIVED MANY AWARDS. THE HONOR THAT MEANT THE MOST TO HIM WAS FROM SIMPSON COLLEGE.

PEOPLE FROM ALL AROUND THE WORLD WROTE LETTERS TO CARVER. HE EVEN MET PRESIDENT FRANKLIN DELANO ROOSEVELT, WHO SUFFERED FROM POLIO. CARVER SENT HIM PEANUT OIL TO RUB INTO HIS LEGS.

WELCOME TO TUSKEGEE, PRESIDENT ROOSEVELT.

I WANT TO THANK YOU FOR THE OIL YOU SENT ME AND FOR THE WORK YOU DO FOR PEOPLE WITH POLIO.

CARVER'S WORK IMPRESSED OTHER AMERICAN INVENTORS. IT IS SAID THAT THOMAS EDISON OFFERED HIM A JOB. HENRY FORD, THE CARMAKER, BECAME CARVER'S FRIEND.

I THINK THAT PROFESSOR CARVER IS ONE OF THE WORLD'S GREATEST LIVING SCIENTISTS.

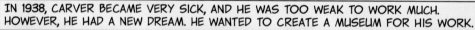

IN 1938, CARVER BECAME VERY SICK, AND HE WAS TOO WEAK TO WORK MUCH. HOWEVER, HE HAD A NEW DREAM. HE WANTED TO CREATE A MUSEUM FOR HIS WORK.

PEOPLE ALWAYS WRITE TO ME ABOUT MY EXPERIMENTS AND WORK. I WOULD LIKE THEM TO SEE IT FOR THEMSELVES WHEN I AM GONE.

IT WOULD BE AN HONOR TO HAVE YOUR MUSEUM AT TUSKEGEE. HENRY FORD HAS EVEN SENT US MONEY FOR IT.

THE GEORGE WASHINGTON CARVER MUSEUM OPENED IN 1939. THE BUILDING IT WAS IN WAS ONCE THE LAUNDRY ROOM FOR TUSKEGEE INSTITUTE.

AFTER ALL THE WASHING I DID IN MY LIFE, IT IS FITTING THAT MY MUSEUM IS IN A LAUNDRY!

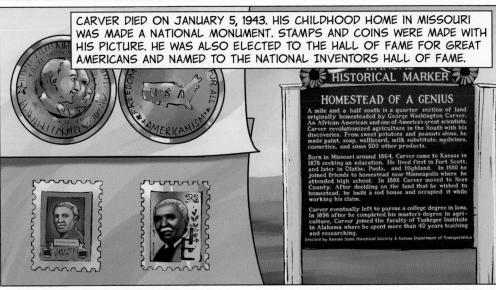

CARVER DIED ON JANUARY 5, 1943. HIS CHILDHOOD HOME IN MISSOURI WAS MADE A NATIONAL MONUMENT. STAMPS AND COINS WERE MADE WITH HIS PICTURE. HE WAS ALSO ELECTED TO THE HALL OF FAME FOR GREAT AMERICANS AND NAMED TO THE NATIONAL INVENTORS HALL OF FAME.

HISTORICAL MARKER

HOMESTEAD OF A GENIUS

A mile and a half south is a quarter section of land originally homesteaded by George Washington Carver. An African American and one of America's great scientists. Carver revolutionized agriculture in the South with his discoveries. From sweet potatoes and peanuts alone, he made paint, soap, wallboard, milk substitute, medicines, cosmetics, and some 500 other products.

Born in Missouri around 1864, Carver came to Kansas in 1878 seeking an education. He lived first in Fort Scott, and later in Olathe, Paola, and Highland. In 1880 he joined friends to homestead near Minneapolis where he attended high school. In 1886 Carver moved to Ness County. After deciding on the land that he wished to homestead, he built a sod house and occupied it while working his claim.

Carver eventually left to pursue a college degree in Iowa. In 1896 after he completed his master's degree in agriculture, Carver joined the faculty of Tuskegee Institute in Alabama where he spent more than 40 years teaching and researching.

Erected by Kansas State Historical Society & Kansas Department of Transportation

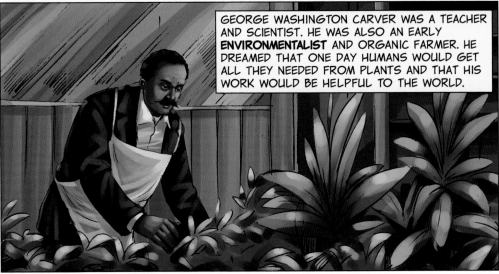

GEORGE WASHINGTON CARVER WAS A TEACHER AND SCIENTIST. HE WAS ALSO AN EARLY **ENVIRONMENTALIST** AND ORGANIC FARMER. HE DREAMED THAT ONE DAY HUMANS WOULD GET ALL THEY NEEDED FROM PLANTS AND THAT HIS WORK WOULD BE HELPFUL TO THE WORLD.

Timeline

c. 1864 or 1865	George Carver is born on a farm near Diamond Grove, Missouri. The exact date is not known.
1877	Carver leaves home to go to school in Neosho, Missouri.
1878–1884	Carver moves around Kansas, attending various schools and earning money by doing laundry.
1885	Highland College turns down Carver because he is African American.
1886–1889	Carver homesteads in western Kansas, then moves to Iowa after a great blizzard.
1890	Carver enrolls at Simpson College.
1891	Carver transfers to Iowa State Agricultural College and studies agriculture.
1894	Carver earns his bachelor's degree in agriculture.
1896	Carver earns his master's degree from Iowa State and serves on the faculty.
1896	Carver goes to Tuskegee Institute as the school's director of the Department of Agriculture.
1916	Carver is elected a fellow of the Royal Society of Arts in London, England.
1921	Carver speaks in front of the US House of Representatives to support the peanut industry.
1923	Carver receives the Spingarn Medal from the National Association for the Advancement of Colored People (NAACP).
1928	Simpson College awards Carver an honorary doctor of science degree.
1938	Carver becomes very sick. He raises money for a museum, which opens the following year.
1943	George Washington Carver dies in Tuskegee, Alabama.

Glossary

agriculture (A-grih-kul-cher) The science of producing crops and raising livestock, or animals.

biofuel (by-oh-FYOOL) Something made out of natural, raw materials that is used to make power.

can (KAN) To preserve by putting in airtight jars or other containers.

chamomile (KA-muh-my-el) An herb whose flower heads are dried and used to make tea.

Civil War (SIH-vul WOR) The war fought between the Northern and the Southern states of America from 1861 to 1865.

compost (KOM-pohst) A mixture of decaying matter, such as leaves, used as a fertilizer.

environmentalist (in-vy-run-MEN-tuh-lust) Someone who wants to keep the natural world safe.

fertile (FER-tul) Good for making and growing things.

fertilizer (FUR-tuh-lyz-er) Something put in soil to help crops grow.

healer (HEE-lur) Someone who helps sick people feel better.

homesteader (HOHM-steh-der) A person who settles on land granted by the government under the Homestead Act.

hybrid (HY-brud) The offspring of two different kinds of plants.

industrial (in-DUS-tree-ul) Having to do with the production of goods.

manufacture (man-yuh-FAK-cher) To make something by hand or with a machine.

manure (muh-NUHR) Animal waste that is used on farms to help crops grow.

Negroes (NEE-grohz) African Americans. The term is no longer used.

nutrients (NOO-tree-unts) Food that a living thing needs to live and grow.

prejudice (PREH-juh-dis) Disliking a group of people different from you.

products (PRAH-dukts) Things that are produced.

rejection (ree-JEK-shun) The act of turning something or someone down.

rotation (roh-TAY-shun) Changing a fixed order.

thrive (THRYV) To grow strong or well.

Index

Websites

Due to the changing nature of Internet links, PowerKids Press has developed an online list of websites related to the subject of this book. This site is updated regularly. Please use this link to access the list:

www.powerkidslinks.com/jgai/carv/